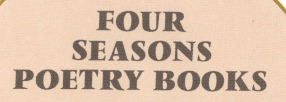

FOUR SEASONS POETRY BOOKS

AUTUMN

COMPILED BY JENNIFER WILSON

ILLUSTRATED BY GRAHAM COOPER

Macdonald Children's Books

Contents

Introduction

Have you ever watched a blacksmith at work? Sometimes he turns a rod of iron into a delicate twisted pattern or an animal's head, like the ram's head which I have on a poker. But, however delicate the final shape might be, the metal has to be heated through red to white hot and then hammered very hard on the anvil which makes the special ringing sound of the forge.

A poet is like a smith working with words. To achieve just the right rhythm or rhyme, or shape or sound or meaning he has to hammer away at words. He works hard so that the words are hard working too. There is no space in a poem for an extra word with nothing to do and those that are finally chosen often do many jobs. Each time we read a poem we may see a new meaning or picture as we realise how many ways the words can be understood. So a poem is like a Jack-in-the-box; we all know what is there but each time it is released it is a surprise and moves in a new way.

The poems here are like that for me. Stand in the 'forge' alongside these authors and find out how they work. They are all about Autumn, or feel like Autumn to me. Perhaps you will not agree. Look out for witches abroad on Hallowe'en!

Jennifer Wilson

Midas

'The touch of gold!'
King Midas boldy craved.
Eyes glittered as he ran
from Bacchus' mountain cave
to find a golden land
where purple grape and twig of oak,
sleek lizard, stone and waving corn
like golden apples of the sun
all gilded to his stroke.

'A golden future!'
Midas cried
upon his golden throne.
And scarlet rose with olive branch,
plump aubergine and fragrant grass
passed through his grasping Judas kiss
to dazzle in the sun.

'Bring on the feast!'
King Midas laughed,
reached out for wine and bread;
raised his glass to take a sip
but when the red wine touched his lip
King Midas understood.

Oh gold was my corn and green my vine
and red was my wine of old;
never again shall I pine for wealth
or crave a richer world.

Lord Bacchus took pity, freed the king
from the gift he had longed to hold;
yet Autumn comes still with its Midas touch,
turns all to dying gold.

Judith Nicholls

5

Listen

Silence is when you can hear things.
Listen:
The breathing of bees,
A moth's footfall,
Or the mist easing its way
Across the field,
The light shifting at dawn
Or the stars clicking into place
At evening.

John Cotton

The Mouse in the Wainscot

Hush, Suzanne!
Don't lift your cup.
That breath you heard
Is a mouse getting up.

As the mist that steams
From your milk as you sup,
So soft is the sound
Of a mouse getting up.

There! did you hear
His feet pitter-patter
Lighter than tipping
Of beads on a platter,

And then like a shower
On the window pane
The little feet scampering
Back again?

O falling of feather!
O drift of a leaf!
The mouse in the wainscot
Is dropping asleep.

Ian Serraillier

First Day at School

A millionbillionwillion miles from home
Waiting for the bell to go. (To go where?)
Why are they all so big, other children?
So noisy? So much at home they
must have been born in uniform
Lived all their lives in playgrounds
Spent the years inventing games
that don't let me in. Games
that are rough, that swallow you up.

And the railings.
All around, the railings.
Are they to keep out wolves and monsters?
Things that carry off and eat children?
Things you don't take sweets from?
Perhaps they're to stop us getting out
Running away from the lessins. Lessin.
What does a lessin look like?
Sounds small and slimy.
They keep them in glassrooms.
Whole rooms made out of glass. Imagine.

I wish I could remember my name
Mummy said it would come in useful.
Like wellies. When there's puddles.
Lellowwellies. I wish she was here.
I think my name is sewn on somewhere
Perhaps the teacher will read it for me.
Tea-cher. The one who makes the tea.

Roger McGough

One Day of Autumn

One day of autumn
sun had uncongealed
the frost that clung
wherever shadows spread
their arctic greys among
October grass: mid-
field an oak still
held its foliage intact
but then began
releasing leaf by leaf
full half,
till like a startled
flock they scattered
on the wind: and one
more venturesome than all
the others shone far out
a moment in mid-air,
before it glittered off
and sheered into the dip
a stream ran through
to disappear with it

Charles Tomlinson

To an Oak Dropping Acorns

With my two arms I cannot span thy girth,
Yet when I pick thy acorn from the earth
Within my hand I hold a ship at sea,
My bed, my table, and my own roof-tree.

Eleanor Farjeon

A Sheep Fair

The day arrives of the autumn fair,
    And torrents fall,
Though sheep in throngs are gathered there,
    Ten thousand all,
Sodden, with hurdles round them reared:
And, lot by lot, the pens are cleared,
And the auctioneer wrings out his beard,
And wipes his book, bedrenched and smeared,
And rakes the rain from his face with the edge of his hand,
    As torrents fall.

The wool of the ewes is like a sponge
    With the daylong rain:
Jammed tight, to turn, or lie, or lunge,
    They strive in vain.
Their horns are soft as finger-nails,
Their shepherds reek against the rails,
The tied dogs soak with tucked-in tails,
The buyers' hat-brims fill like pails,
Which spill small cascades when they shift their stand
    In the daylong rain.

Thomas Hardy

Harvest Home

The wagons loom like blue caravans in the dusk:
they lumber mysteriously down the moonlit lanes.

We ride on the stacks of rust gold corn
filling the sky with our song.

The horses toss their heads and the harness-bells
jingle all the way.

Herbert Read

Conkers

When chestnuts are hanging
Above the school yard,
They are little green sea-mines
Spiky and hard.

But when they fall bursting
And all the boys race,
Each shines like a jewel
In a satin case.

Clive Sansom

14

To a Conker

Glossy horse-chestnut
foal, if you do not today
fall on luck &
found a horse-
chestnut tree, tomorrow
will have you defeated,
meagre, matt-coated,
unsheltered, shrunk, bony-ribbed, and, perhaps,
tied to a string; – so
land on Good Luck; conquer!

Gerda Mayer

Only the Moon

When I was a child I thought
The new moon was a cradle
The full moon was granny's round face.

The new moon was a banana
The full moon was a big cake.

When I was a child
I never saw the moon
I only saw what I wanted to see.

And now I see the moon
It's the moon
Only the moon, and nothing but the moon.

Wong May

Moonscape

No air, no mist, no man, no beast.
No water flows from her Sea of Showers,
no trees, no flowers fringe her Lake of Dreams.
No grass grows or clouds shroud her high hills
or deep deserts. No whale blows in her dry
                              Ocean of Storms.

Judith Nicholls

Psalm 65 Verses 9-13

Thou visitest the earth and waterest it,
Thou greatly enrichest it;
The river of God is full of water:
Thou providest them corn, when thou hast so prepared the earth.
Thou waterest her furrows abundantly;
Thou settlest the ridges thereof:
Thou makest it soft with showers;
Thou blessest the springing thereof.
Thou crownest the year with thy goodness;
And thy paths drop fatness.
They drop upon the pastures of the wilderness:
And the hills are girded with joy.
The pastures are clothed with flocks;
The valleys also are covered with corn;
They shout for joy, they also sing.

from The Holy Bible, Authorized Version

The Wasp

Where the ripe pears droop heavily
   The yellow wasp hums loud and long
   His hot and drowsy autumn song:
A yellow flame he seems to be,
   When darting suddenly from high
   He lights where fallen peaches lie:
Yellow and black this tiny thing's
A tiger soul on elfin wings.

William Sharp

Cold Feet

They have all gone across
They are all turning to see
They are all shouting 'come on'
They are all waiting for me.

I look through the gaps in the footway
And my heart shrivels with fear,
For far below the river is flowing
So quick and so cold and so clear.

And all that there is between it
And me falling down there is this:
A few wooden planks – not very thick –
And between each, a little abyss.

The holes get right under my sandals.
I can see straight through to the rocks,
And if I don't look, I can feel it,
Just there, through my shoes and my socks.

Suppose my feet and my legs withered up
And slipped through the slats like a rug?
Suppose I suddenly went very thin
Like the baby that slid down the plug?

I know that it cannot happen
But suppose that it did, what then?
Would they be able to find me
And take me back home again?

They have all gone across
They are all waiting to see
They are all shouting 'come on' –
But they'll have to carry me.

Brian Lee

Horse Chestnuts

Autumn's special toys,
There is something about the newness of them,
Their gloss, the colour of burnished horses,
Their richness protected from their fall
By those thick green cases,
So that we can harvest them
Safe in their nests
Of last year's debris of leaves,
To pocket them
For treasure or for play.
Though they will never be
Quite so beautiful again,
As that first moment
When we saw them peep pristine
From their soft-spiked shells.

John Cotton

Bilberries

on the hillside
in shaggy coats
hobgoblin fruit
easy for little
hands

Gerda Mayer

The Old Stone House

Nothing on the grey roof, nothing on the brown,
Only a little greening where the rain drips down;
Nobody at the window, nobody at the door,
Only a little hollow which a foot once wore;
But still I tread on tiptoe, still tiptoe on I go,
Past nettles, porch, and weedy well, for oh, I know
A friendless face is peering, and a clear still eye
Peeps closely through the casement as my step goes by.

Walter de la Mare

The Shed

There's a shed at the bottom of our garden
With a spider's web hanging across the door,
The hinges are rusty and creak in the wind.
When I'm in bed I lie and I listen,
I'll open that door one day.

There's a dusty old window around at the side
With three cracked panes of glass,
I often think there's someone staring at me
Each time that I pass,
I'll peep through that window one day.

My brother says there's a ghost in the shed
Who hides under the rotten floorboards,
And if I ever dare to set foot inside
He'll jump out and chop off my head,
But I'll take a peek one day.

I know that there isn't really a ghost,
My brother tells lies to keep the shed for his den;
There isn't anyone staring or making strange noises
And the spider has been gone from his web since I don't
    know when,
I'll go into that shed one day soon,

But not just yet . . .

Frank Flynn

25

The Hedgehog

There's a hedgehog in the garden – come and see.
When he's still, he's like a pincushion that breathes.
When he moves, he's like a fat freckled mouse, following me
All over the place with pitter-patter feet.
He snorts and snuffs and sniffs my shoe,
Then hauls himself over the rise.

We'll introduce him to the cat. But she runs away
Into the box-tree, all hidden save her eyes
And nose and twitching tail –
Then suddenly leaps out and pounces.
(Can you blame her? He's drunk all
Her saucerful of milk, three fluid ounces.)

Caught?
Not likely. She pulls up short
And dances and prances and saws
The air all round him, mighty dainty with her paws;
Then, defeated, slinks away
To sulk or chase less prickly prey.

It's chilly now and getting late.
We'll cover him with a pile of autumn leaves
And let him hide or even hibernate.
In the morning we'll creep
Over the lawn and part the leaves and peer
Inside, and see if he's lying there asleep.
I hope he is . . .

Ian Serraillier

The Ride-By-Nights

Up on their brooms the Witches stream,
Crooked and black in the crescent's gleam;
One foot high, and one foot low,
Bearded, cloaked, and cowled, they go.

'Neath Charlie's Wane they twitter and tweet,
And away they swarm 'neath the Dragon's feet,
With a whoop and a flutter they swing and sway,
And surge pell-mell down the Milky Way.

Between the legs of the glittering Chair
They hover and squeak in the empty air.
Then round they swoop past the glimmering Lion
To where Sirius barks behind huge Orion;
Up, then, and over to wheel amain
Under the silver, and home again.

28   Walter de la Mare

The Witches' Ride

Over the hills
Where the edge of light
Deepens and darkens
To ebony night,
Narrow hats high
Above yellow bead eyes,
The tatter-haired witches
Ride through the skies.
Over the seas
Where the flat fishes sleep
Wrapped in the slap of the slippery deep,
Over the peaks
Where the black trees are bare,
Where the boney birds quiver
They glide through the air.
Silently humming
A horrible tune,
They sweep through the stillness
To sit on the moon.

Karla Kushkin

The Last Leaf

I saw how rows of white raindrops
    From bare boughs shone,
And how the storm had stript the leaves
    Forgetting none
Save one left high on a top twig
    Swinging alone;
Then that too bursting into song
    Fled and was gone.

Andrew Young

Autumn

Wanting to go,
all the leaves want to go
though they have achieved
their kingly robes.

Weary of colours,
they think of black earth,
they think of
white snow.

Stealthily, delicately
as a safebreaker
they unlock themselves
from branches.

And from their royal towers
they sift silently down
to become part of
the proletariat of mud.

Norman MacCaig

Acknowledgements

Culford Books wish to thank the following for their kind permission to use their material:

'Listen' and 'Horse Chestnuts' John Cotton from THE CRYSTAL ZOO by John Cotton, L.J. Anderson and U.A. Fanthorpe (1985) Oxford University Press. 'The Old Stone House' and 'The Ride-By-Nights' Walter de la Mare by permission of The Literary Trustees of Walter de la Mare and The Society of Authors as their representative. 'To an Oak Dropping Acorns' Eleanor Farjeon from INVITATION TO A MOUSE Hodder & Stoughton. 'The Shed' Frank Flynn from THE CANDY-FLOSS TREE: poems of Gerda Mayer, Frank Flynn, & Norman Nicholson (1984) Oxford University Press. 'The Witches' Ride' from DOGS & DRAGONS, TREES & DREAMS: A Collection of Poems by Karla Kuskin Copyright © 1964 by Karla Kuskin. Reprinted by permission of Harper & Row, Publishers, Inc. 'Cold Feet' Brian Lee from LATE HOME (Kestral Books, 1976), page 22, copyright © 1976 by Brian Lee reproduced by permission of Penguin Books Ltd. 'Autumn' Norman MacCaig from COLLETED POEMS BY NORMAN MACCAIG Chatto & Windus. 'First Day At School' Roger McGough from IN THE GLASSROOM Jonathan Cape. 'Only the Moon' Wong May from SEVEN POETS, SINGAPORE AND MALAYSIA Singapore University Press Pte. 'To a Conker' Gerda Mayer from THE KNOCKABOUT SHOW Chatto & Windus. 'Bilberries' Gerda Mayer from THE CANDY-FLOSS TREE: poems by Gerda Mayer, Frank Flynn, & Norman Nicholson (1984) Oxford University Press. 'Midas', 'Moonscape' Judith Nicholls from MAGIC MIRROR Faber & Faber. 'Harvest Home' Herbert Read from COLLECTED POEMS Faber & Faber. 'Conkers' Clive Sansom from THE GOLDEN UNICORN Methuen. 'The Mouse in the Wainscot' © 1950 Ian Serraillier, and Oxford University Press. 'The Hedgehog' © 1963 Ian Serraillier, and Oxford University Press. 'One Day of Autumn' Charles Tomlinson from CHARLES TOMLINSON'S COLLECTED POEMS (1985) Oxford University Press. 'The Last Leaf' Andrew Young from THE POETICAL WORKS OF ANDREW YOUNG Martin Secker ·Warburg.

A MACDONALD CHILDREN'S BOOK

This collection of poetry © Jennifer Wilson 1987
Introduction © Jennifer Wilson 1987
Illustration © Graham Cooper 1987
FOUR SEASONS POETRY BOOKS © Culford Books 1987

First published in Great Britain in 1987 by
Macdonald & Company (Publishers) Ltd
This edition Macdonald Children's Books
Simon & Schuster International Group
Reprinted 1989
All rights reserved

Conceived, edited, designed and produced by Culford Books,
Sunningwell House, Sunningwell, Abingdon,
Oxfordshire OX 13 6RD
Edited by Penelope Miller
Designed by Judith Allan
Photoset by Lantern Graphics Ltd

Printed and bound in Great Britain by
BPCC Paulton Books Limited

Macdonald Children's Books
Simon & Schuster International Group
Wolsey House, Wolsey Road,
Hemel Hempstead HP2 4SS

British Library Cataloguing in Publication Data

Autumn. —— (Four seasons poetry).
1. Autumn —— Juvenile poetry 2. Children's
poetry, English
I. Wilson, Jennifer II. Cooper, Graham
III. Series
821'.008'033   PZ8.3

ISBN 0-7500-0041-4